Liszt Masterpieces
for Solo Piano
13 Works

FRANZ LISZT

Edited by
Ferruccio Busoni, Emil von Sauer,
José Vianna da Motta and Yakov Mil'shteyn

DOVER PUBLICATIONS, INC.
Mineola, New York

Bibliographical Note

This Dover edition, first published in 2000, is a new compilation of thirteen piano works originally published separately in early authoritative editions. The annotated contents list is newly added. Stanley Appelbaum provided the English translations of the poems on pp. 42 and 58 specially for this edition.
We are indebted to Dr. Alan Walker, McMaster University, Hamilton, Ontario, for clarifying the background information on the works in this edition. Thanks, too, to Prof. Donald Manildi, International Piano Archives at Maryland, University of Maryland at College Park, for providing a rare early edition of the two Concert Études.

International Standard Book Number: 0-486-41379-9

Manufactured in the United States of America
Dover Publications, Inc., 31 East 2nd Street, Mineola, N.Y. 11501

CONTENTS

Titles are given in the language most commonly associated with the music. Dual catalogue numbers "R" and "S" are found in two standard reference works: Peter Raabe's *Franz Liszt: Leben und Schaffen* (1931, 1968), and Humphrey Searle's *The Music of Liszt* (1954, 1966).

Rákóczy March
(Hungarian Rhapsody No. 15 in A Minor) 104

Liszt's famous arrangement of Hungary's national "call to arms," associated with Prince
Ferenc Rákóczy II (1676–1735), who was the first leader of the fight for Hungarian inde-
pendence against the Habsburgs (1703–1711). This is the second (1871) of three versions,
based on themes from Liszt's sets of Hungarian national melodies (*Magyar Dallok*) and
rhapsodies (*Magyar Rhapsodiák*), and from his symphonic arrangement of the march
(1865). • R106 / S244

Nuages Gris 116

"Gray Clouds" (1881): This work has been described as 'a gateway to modern music',
acquiring in recent years the status of an icon among Liszt aficionados. With its advanced
harmonies, and its unresolved ending that drifts away into keylessness, the piece foretells
the coming of impressionism in music. The "Gray Clouds" were evidently autobiographical
in origin. In early August 1881, Liszt suffered a fall down the stairs of the Hofgärtnerei, his
occasional home in Weimar. His injuries were severe enough to keep him in bed for the
next several weeks. The music depicts a world of quiet desolation. The manuscript bears
the date 24 August 1881. • R78 / S199

Valse Oubliée No. 1 118

"Forgotten Waltz No. 1" (1881): the first of *Quatre Valses Oubliées*. • R37 / S215

Hungarian Rhapsody No. 2
in C-sharp Minor

Edited by Yakov Mil'shteyn

poco a poco accelerando il tempo

sempre p

stringendo con strepito

Un Sospiro
Concert Étude No. 3 in D-flat Major

Allegro affettuoso.   Edited by Ferruccio Busoni

*) Die nach unten gestrichenen Noten sind mit der linken, die nach oben gestrichenen mit der rechten Hand zu spielen.
On jouera avec la main gauche les notes dont la queue est descendante, avec la droite celles dont la queue est ascendante.
The notes with stems pointing downwards are to be played with the left, those with stems pointing upwards, with the right hand.

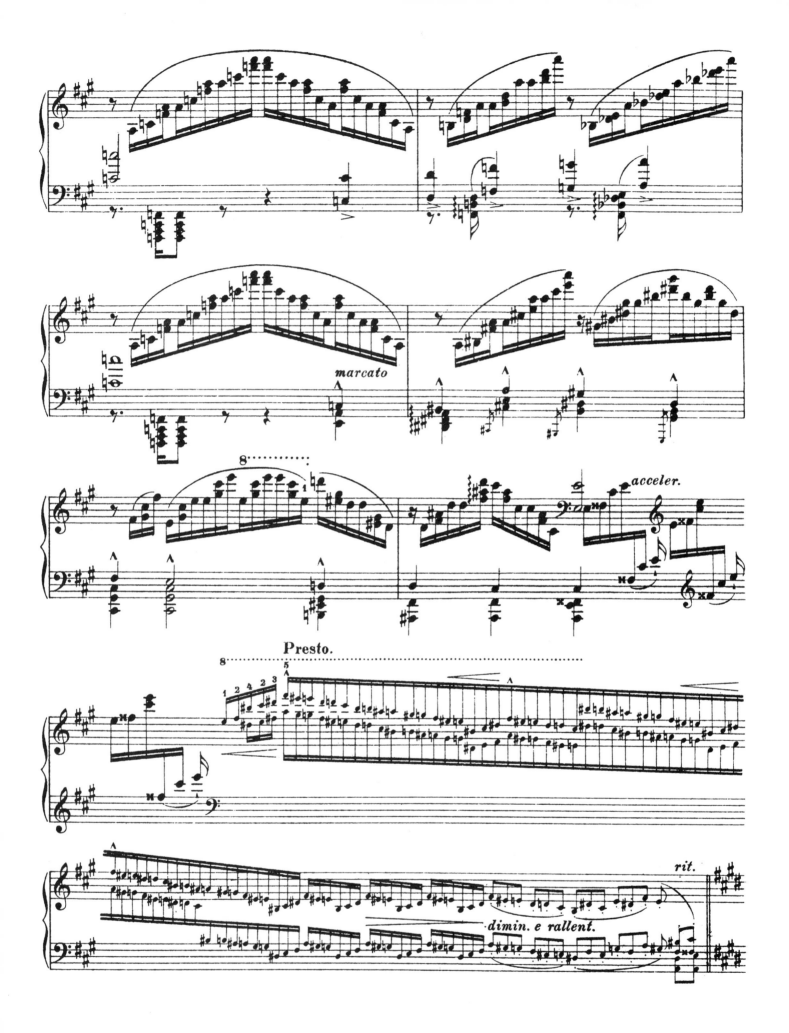

Funérailles, Octobre 1849

Harmonies Poétiques et Religieuses / No. 7

Edited by José Vianna da Motta

Allegro energico assai.

Consolation No. 3

in D-flat Major

Lento placido.

Edited by José Vianna da Motta

Cantando

Liebestraum No. 3

from *Liebesträume, 3 Notturnos*
(Dreams of Love, 3 Nocturnes)

Poem by Ferdinand Freiligrath
English translation by Stanley Appelbaum

O LIEB
(Oh, Love)

O lieb, o lieb so lang du lieben kannst, so
    lang du lieben magst.
    Die Stunde kommt, wo du an Gräbern
    stehst und klagst.
Und sorge dass dein Herze glüht, und Liebe
    hegt und Liebe trägt,
    So lang ihm noch ein ander Herz in Liebe
    warm entgegenschlägt.

Und wer dir seine Brust Erschliesst, o tu ihm
    was du kannst zu lieb
    Und mach ihm jede Stunde froh, und
    mach ihm keine Stunde trüb!
Und hüte deine Zunge wohl: bald ist ein
    hartes Wort entflohn.
    O Gott—es war nicht bös gemeint—
    Der andre aber geht und weint.

Oh, love, oh love as long as you can love, as
    long as you wish to love.
    The hour will come when you stand by
    graves and lament.
And take care that your heart glows, and
    harbors love and bears love,
    As long as another heart still beats in
    return, warm with love.

And whoever uncovers your heart, oh, do all
    the lovable things for him you can,
    And make every hour happy for him, and
    make no hour dreary for him!
And watch your tongue carefully: a harsh
    word escapes all too quickly.
    Oh, God—it wasn't meant to be cruel—
    But the other walks away and weeps.

Liebestraum No. 3

in A-flat Major

Edited by Emil von Sauer

To Clara Schumann

La Campanella

Grande Étude de Paganini No. 3

Edited by Ferruccio Busoni

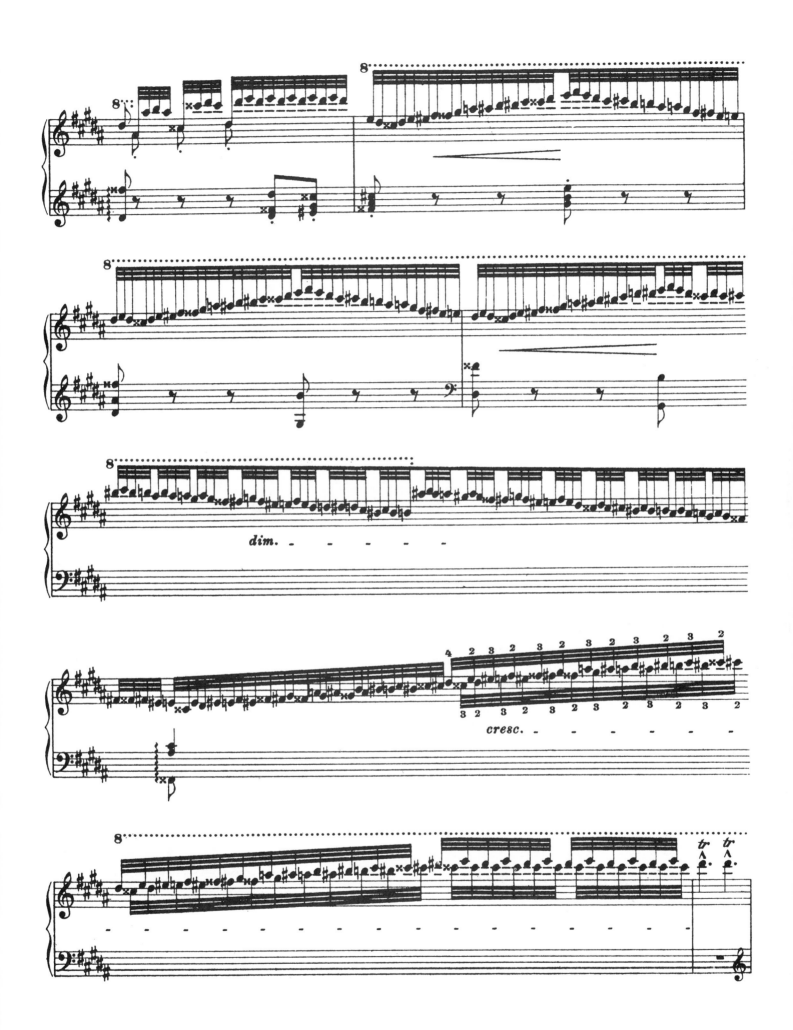

Sonetto 104 del Petrarca

Petrarch's Sonnet 104
English translation by Stanley Appelbaum

Pace non trovo, e non ho da far guerra;
E temo e spero, ed ardo e son un ghiaccio,
E volo sopra 'l cielo e giaccio in terra;
E nullo stringo, e tutto il mondo abbraccio.

Tal m'ha in prigion, che non m'apre, né serra;
Né per suo mi riten, né scioglie il laccio;
E non m'ancide Amor, e non mi sferra;
Né mi vuol vivo, né mi trae d'impaccio.

Veggio senz' occhi; e non ho lingua e grido,
E bramo di perir, e cheggio aita;
Ed ho in idio me stesso ed amo altrui:

Pascomi di dolor, piangendo rido;
Equalmente mi spiace morte e vita.
In questo stato son, Donna, per Vui.

I can't find peace, and have no war to wage;
I fear and hope, I blaze and I'm like ice;
I fly higher than the sky and I lie on the ground;
I clasp nothing, and I embrace the whole world.

I'm kept a prisoner by one who neither opens nor locks my cell;
She neither claims me for her own, nor loosens my bonds;
Love neither kills me nor undoes my chains;
He doesn't want me to live, but doesn't remove my distress.

I see without eyes; I have no tongue and I clamor,
I yearn to perish, and I call for aid;
I loathe myself and I love another:

I feed on sorrow, as I weep I laugh;
I'm equally displeased with death and life.
I'm in this condition, my lady, on your account.

Sonetto 104 del Petrarca

Années de Pèlerinage, Deuxième Année: Italie / No. 5

Edited by Yakov Mil'shteyn

To Carl Tausig

Mephisto Waltz No. 1
"The Dance in the Village Inn"

Edited by Emil von Sauer

*) Mit diesen Ziffern deutet Liszt die rhythmische Betonung an | **) Par ces chiffres Liszt indique l'accentuation rythmique* | **)* Liszt uses these figures to indicate the rhythmical accentuation

64

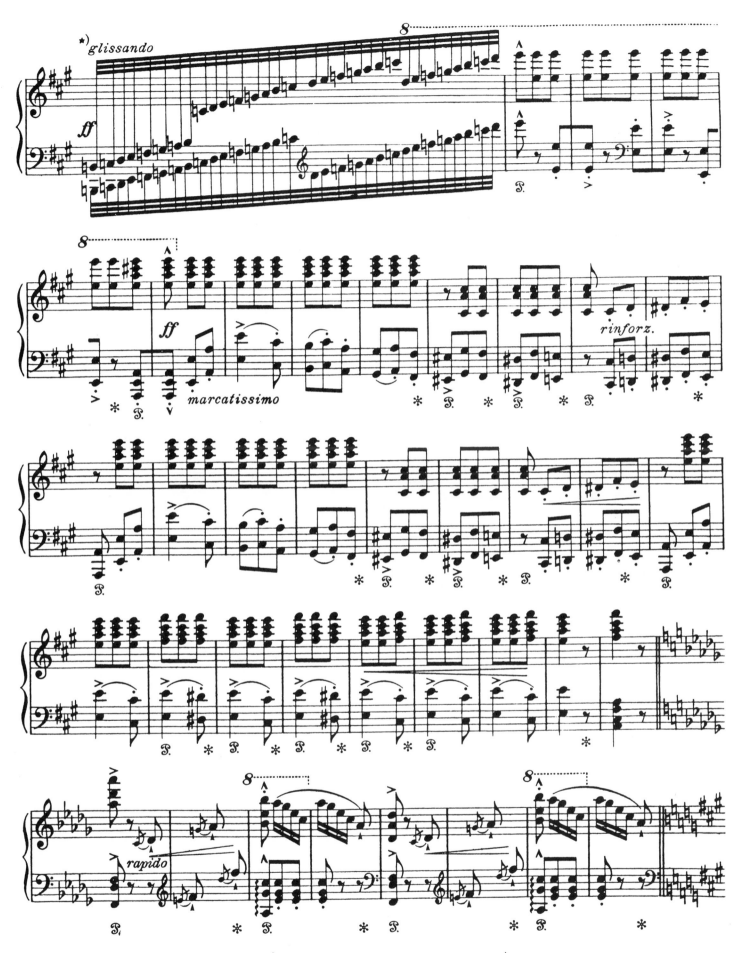

*) Ein hübscher Effekt ist,diesen Lauf
nur in der rechten Hand *glissando*, in
der Linken aber als *Skala* zu spielen.

*) *Il est d'un très bel effet d'exécuter ce
passage* glissando *de la main droite,et
en gamme de la main gauche.*

*)A fine effect is produced by playing
this run *glissando* with the right hand,the
left hand executing it as a *scale*.

Mephisto Waltz No. 1 / 69

*) Die Punkte bedeuten hier kein Wiederan - | *) Ces points ne signifient pas un nouveau | *) These dots do not mean a new touch of the
schlagen der Note, sondern Abheben der Hand. | toucher de la note, mais qu'il faut lever la main. | note but that the hand should be lifted off.

Presto

*) ∧ Bezeichnung für 𝄐𝅘𝅥 bezw. 𝄐𝅘𝅥 | *) ∧ Indication pour 𝄐𝅘𝅥 ou 𝄐𝅘𝅥 | *) ∧ Designation for 𝄐𝅘𝅥 or 𝄐𝅘𝅥

Waldesrauschen
Concert Étude No. 1

Edited by Ferruccio Busoni

88

To Dionys Prukner

Gnomenreigen
Concert Étude No. 2

Edited by Ferruccio Busoni

To Count László Teleky

Rákóczy March
Hungarian Rhapsody No. 15 in A Minor

Allegro animato

Edited by Yakov Mil'shteyn

Tempo di marcia animato

ff marcatissimo

sempre ff

ff

p

Nuages Gris

Valse Oubliée No. 1

Edited by Emil von Sauer